CU00801948

New Life

True Stories From Local People

New Life

Some True Stories From Local People

Compiled by Hywel George

ANCHOR PRINTS

ISBN: 9798341124196

In memory of Colin Ladd. He served well and gained an excellent standing and great assurance in his faith in Christ Jesus.

To the people of Maesycwmmer.

I hope you fill a library with books like this one.

Contents

Preface   i

Carol Jones   1

Chris Pugh   5

Emily Lewis   11

Paul Young   16

Heddina Stephens   19

Mike Williams   24

Jill Jones   30

Heddwen George   31

John Price   36

Epilogue   39

Preface

If you are interested in the lives of your neighbours, what is distinctive about them and what makes them tick, then this is a book you will want to read. In it, you will read some short stories written by local people (some of whom may be well-known to you) in which they describe a new start in life for them.

Have you ever wished you could have a new start in life, or thought if you were starting over you would cut a different path, or maybe choose different companions along the way? Then listen to some of your neighbours as they tell how they discovered a path worth following.

David George

Maesycwmmer, 2024

Never Left Alone

Carol Jones

Maesycwmmer

St Catwg's Church in Gelligaer was very active in the community while I was growing up, and I always went to their Sunday School as a child. Infact, the church was the background to a lot of my social life then. I was usually there on my own though because my parents never really went to church, even if they did respect all its formalities and culture.

As far as I can remember, my life was just normal. I was loved and always had a healthy routine around home, school and church. However, the thing is, I was merely a textbook Christian, nominal.

What does that mean exactly? Well, I read the words from the Bible, I said prayers and went to church on Sundays. I didn't do all the bad things others did and thought well of my polite and respectable self. I called myself a Christian, but the missing piece was the only piece that really mattered: I didn't know

Jesus Christ in my heart. It was all a show. I had the outward appearances of some sort of Christianity but didn't have Christ.

When my husband and I moved to Maesycwmmer with a growing family, I wanted our three boys to go to the local church, Mt Pleasant. I was keen for this because church life, even if it was just in name only, had always been good for me. When I took the boys to Sunday School, I found that the pastor, Malcolm Jones, held an adult Bible Class at the same time. So, for a while, we would go to church together – my boys to the Sunday School and myself to the adult Bible Class.

One Sunday afternoon, the pastor was teaching us from the book of Romans. As part of his lesson, he referred to the wide road which was open to those who will not believe in Jesus, and the narrow road open to those who will believe in Jesus: a road which leads to the glory of God.

I had not expected this at all, but I just knew instantly, deep down in myself, that I desperately did not want to be on that wide road which leads to destruction. I had heard similar things to this for a very long time, but it was there and then that the Holy Spirit opened my heart to it all and I knew it was true. I confessed in that session that I had finally accepted Jesus Christ was my Saviour and Lord.

The old way of things was suddenly gone. No more outward show and 'Christianity without Christ'. Now I was a real Christian, with Jesus in my heart. I knew he had died to save not just any old people but even ME from my sins, even the sins of hypocritically playing like a Christian for most of my life. In short, he had given me new life!

That day was many years ago. I've been a member of Mt Pleasant Church ever since, nearly 45 years. During that time, life has not been without its challenges. Some of those difficulties have been part and parcel of usual life experiences, and some of them have been the direct result of being a Christian. Nevertheless, having the Lord Jesus with me means I have never been alone to face a single one of them because he promised me, 'I am with you always.'

When Jesus came into my heart, he made me know his unconditional love for me. He gave me his own peace and strength which has never left me, and it never will. He helped me through a major cancer operation and has been supporting me through the last 13 years of widowhood. He even helped me when I downsized from the family home to where I live now. These were huge challenges for me but through them all, Jesus was very close to comfort and encourage me. Psalm 23 says that even when I go through the valley of the shadow of death, he is with me; I have tested and found that promise to be wonderfully and absolutely true!

Wherever you find yourself in life at the moment, or whatever direction your life seems to be taking, take a moment to reflect on these words of Jesus: *'I have told you these things, so that in me you may have peace. In this world you will have trouble. But take heart! I have overcome the world.'*

He Held Me Tight

Chris Pugh

Bargoed

I thought my Mam and Dad were brainwashed. They always bothered me to become a Christian while I was young, reading the Bible to me, praying, and singing hymns around the piano with my brother. I never listened when Dad pleaded with me, 'enter in the narrow gate.' When he took me to hear famous preachers like Martyn Lloyd-Jones, I never understood; it was as if I was deaf.

As I grew old enough to leave home, I looked forward to leaving all that religious stuff behind. I remember saying to God, while on the bus sometime, 'God, this is MY life, and I'm going to live it how I want to!' From then on, I never really thought of him, I didn't want to know. I lived in Cefn Hengoed then, and my life was about me. I did whatever I wanted.

Around 1975, I was going through Cefn Hengoed and spotted some Christians handing out gospel literature and tracts. Don't ask me why, I don't know, I decided to go to church that Sunday. I went and asked one of them, John Morley, who said I could come along to Bethel the next Sunday. I guess I was curious.

That first Sunday I was sitting at the back and prayed, 'Lord, hurry up and save me, I have to get to the Double Diamond with the girls by 8:30pm!' I cared more about getting to that club in Caerphilly than anything about my soul. I attended Bethel for a few months before moving to Bargoed. My heart was still dead cold to the Lord, and I didn't care. Mam sent me a Bible every year for Christmas, and I would pile them up, unopened. I didn't go to church again for about ten years.

By now I was married to Jeff and we were starting a family. The Lord was nobody to me, I lived how I liked. The thing is, I had yet to learn that living my way, for myself, how I liked, was not good for me or anyone else. I had a hot and quick temper. If Jeff was home late from work, he'd know about it. He'd see his dinner hit the floor, or it would already be in the dog. I'd drain his beer down the sink or feed him a dog food pie. I'm ashamed to say it now but this is who I was, so insensitive to my own selfishness and carelessness.

In 1985, my neighbour, Lyn was bereaved of her Aunty Glad. Lyn begged me to go to Glad's funeral, I resisted, but Lyn persuaded me saying that she wanted me to sit beside her in the funeral. When I went along, I was angry to have to squeeze in the back while Lyn was at the front! My temper was quickly checked by what I heard. Something so familiar, but this time, someone was opening my ears.

The preacher at Glad's funeral quoted from the Bible and said that Glad was hearing from the Lord Jesus, *'Well done, thou good and faithful servant.'*

Those words were like a sword into my soul, they convicted me. I was hurting deep, sad, grieved by it because, I thought to myself, 'He won't be saying that to me.' The way that I live, the way that I am, is sinful.

Lyn took me to the cemetery where the mourners wept over Glad, and I wept over my sinful soul.

I think I cried for a week. The Holy Spirit had opened my ears to finally hear what I'd been listening to for so long. All Mam and Dad had told me, all I had heard in Bethel, it had all become real. I believed it all. I was a sinner, only God could save me, and I needed him to! I remember reading Psalm 139 after the funeral and the weight of the truth of the words were overpowering. All those things to which I had been so insensitive were now so potent and forceful to my heart.

The following Monday was Easter Bank Holiday Monday. I knew that there were preaching services in Mt Pleasant Church in Maesycwmmer, and I wanted to go to hear the Bible preached again. But I knew my Mam would be there, so I wanted to go alone and incognito. Jeff took me there and it was packed! Imagine what it was like to find the only seat for me was right next to my Mother! I didn't understand much of the preacher, Donald MacLeod, through his thick Scottish accent. After the service, I confessed to my Mam what had happened to me – she didn't believe me for a while! I had been so decidedly uninterested in Jesus, my own Mother wouldn't believe that I had come to believe in him!

A few weeks later I heard Colin Jones preach from Jeremiah 18:1—10. The prophet Jeremiah sees a potter making a rubbish pot full of mistakes, cracks, scars and mars. I felt that pot was me! Mine was a life ruined by sin, mistakes, selfishness, anger and the rest. The Lord promised to take that pot and, instead of throwing it away like the broken rubbish it was, to remake it whole and good. I was stunned. At that moment I felt as though the Lord had sat me on his lap and was holding me tight. My life, full of ruin and cracks deserved punishment, Hell, the rubbish tip; but he wouldn't throw me away. He loved me, forgave me, and made me whole.

Jeff couldn't miss the transformation in my life. My temper mellowed and I grew in patience. I was flushed with a strange zeal for the Bible which came from outside myself. I would study it every day, pray and attend all the preaching services I could find. I would travel looking for preaching: Tredegar, Crickhowell, everywhere! On the way, I'd have my Bible and would tell anyone and everyone I could find about the love of Jesus for me. Jeff would get an earful all the time too. I was overwhelmed by the truth that God loved me, gave his Son to shed his blood and save me.

I've never looked back. Jesus was so patient with me, telling me the truth all my life. Even when I turned my back on him and ignored him, he still reached out for me. Even in a funeral, he showed me his life, and he's never left me alone. He's made me whole.

I Had Finally Come Home

'Emily Lewis'

Maesycwmmer

Have you ever felt homesick? A deep longing and a heart searching within yourself, yearning for a resting place? I always felt like that, even when I was at home and with my family in Hong Kong. I knew I belonged there but was always conscious of something missing deep down, maybe everyone feels like that.

My homelife was pretty idyllic. I was part of a big family with devoted parents, brothers and sisters. We mostly got on well, looked after and shared with one another, but not one of us knew the Living God of the Bible. He never really came up in conversation. Quite the opposite really. I was brought up to worship pagan gods and the spirits of my ancestors.

I remember going to the temples to offer incense with my family in the vain hope that we would have earned the protection of these powers. The statues of the temple gods used to frighten me, and I actually felt haunted by them.

We didn't think of the true and Living God, but he thought of us all the time, and we didn't know it. He loved me before I knew him, and he was secretly organising things to bring me home. One of the first things he arranged for me was a funeral.

A relative had passed away and their funeral happened to be in a church. Going along was my first time in a church and I wasn't certain what to expect. Like many funerals, it was sad. Emotions were high and people were heartbroken by the loss. Then they sang some hymns, read from the Bible, and prayed to the Living God. As you might imagine, this new experience stirred my searching soul with the deepest questions like, 'What happens after death?' I wouldn't have been able to put it like this at the time, but I was looking for home, the eternal home and rest of my soul. But for all my looking, I was still in the dark.

Questions and longings like these bothered me for a long time. There were no Christians in my family to ask what they thought, but I did have some Christian friends. Looking back, this was another thing which the Lord arranged for my salvation! One Sunday, I asked my friends whether I might go to church with them. This would be my first time going to church on a Sunday.

What happened that day I can never forget. That church service was not like the temples I had always gone to. I heard about Jesus and was overwhelmed by the tangible presence of the Living God. All the lights came on in my heart. I saw the truth in Jesus Christ, repented of my sins and bowed the knee to him.

I felt compelled within myself to run into his loving arms and there, he gave me a peace which is from another world. He literally welcomed me home that Sunday and I knew that I had just joined an eternal and immortal family with the Christians. I was essentially born again, reborn, given new life. I was granted an overwhelming peace within my heart. I

13

had felt homesick all my life until the Living God found me and led me home.

Before that day, I was hopelessly lost and ignorant. I didn't even know I was lost and in need of a Saviour, let alone how lost I was and that that Saviour is Jesus! I was spiritually dead, but that Sunday I was born again and not long later, I was baptised in the name of God the Father, Son and Spirit.

The new peace and joy in my soul from God was absolutely incredible, it completely flooded my heart and I want to shout it to the world! Instead of soul-sickness and yearning for home, I knew Jesus and longed for others to come home to him too. I wanted to share the love of Jesus with everyone I knew, including my family.

One of my sisters didn't come to my baptism but she did see a photo of me being baptised. We got talking about it and I told her how tenderly the Lord Jesus had dealt with my heart. The light started to break into her life too, and that year she also came home to him. The same happened a few years later to another one of my sisters.

My mother had worshipped the false gods and idols all her life. Then, she saw what Jesus did to me and my sisters. She saw that he had given something true, real, lasting and good to us which no other could ever give her. In her final days, she also came home to new life in Jesus. I praise the Lord for his patience and kindness to my mother.

My husband and I moved to Wales and the Lord gave us our sons here. While they were teenagers, the Lord Jesus saved their souls too. One of them was baptised recently in Maesycwmmer. Looking back, I am amazed by his mercy to me and my family, he has always been beside me and will lead me to his heaven, perfect peace.

Jesus said: '*Peace I leave with you; my peace I give you. I do not give to you as the world gives. Do not let your hearts be troubled and do not be afraid.*'

A Battle Began Within Myself

Paul Young

Maesycwmmer

I thought it would be straightforward to give my testimony, and just take a few minutes. But when I tried to write it down, it showed me again the wonders of God's works and how his plan for me came into effect. But here goes!

I was a man of the world. I thought I was in control of my own life and able to solve any problems I encountered. I didn't need help from anyone, since I always felt my own strength was enough. Things started to change for me though, when I was in my thirties. I witnessed the gentle and kind effect of the people at the local fellowship at Mt Pleasant Church and was curious about learning a little more of why they were like they were. They seemed to have an inner peace and humility which I didn't know or understand.

A battle began within myself when I attended some services there. I was angry and, on times, offended by what I heard from the preaching. What I heard was telling me I was a sinner and fell short of God's righteousness. I thought I was surely as good as the next man! Nevertheless, I was still drawn to hear more.

The experience of conversion is different for everyone. Sometimes it's a slow realisation which is not pinpointed at a time, but in my case, it was a blinding moment. I was a firefighter in Newport at the time, and on a night shift with 12 other firefighters. We were in the perfect darkness of our dorm, but I wasn't sleeping. I was fretting and fearful of my lifestyle, realising that Jesus Christ was the only way for the forgiveness and salvation I needed.

I had been looking for peace, but in all the wrong places. I had always been a strong and determined man on the outside, but insecure on the inside. At that moment, I opened my heart and called out to God. Immediately, I no longer felt a broken spirit. I knew I was alone no more and had a Saviour who knew me, even my darkest places, who forgave me, and took my sins away.

That night, I knew a peace within myself which has supported me through the last 40 years. Has my life been sweetness and light ever since? No! Like everyone else, I have endured heartache and pain along with joy and happiness in my life. I have had deep regrets and crises of faith, but through all of this I have never had to face it alone. God has been my constant companion, lifting me up in spirit and faith whenever I have stumbled.

A Deep Peace Inside Myself

Heddina Stephens

Maesycwmmer

I was not long married in 1971 when I saw an advert in the South Wales Echo: 'Houses for Sale, £180 Deposit, Maesycwmmer.' We had exactly £180 in the bank and decided to go for it. Times have changed a lot since then! At the time, I was 19 and had no idea how significant a decision that would turn out to be. We settled so well into the village, we were content, happily married, and began our family here.

Around the time when our children were 2 and 3 years old, I began to feel concerned about their future; any mother does, I suppose. I wanted them to have a good childhood and the best start I could give them. So, I sent them to the Sunday School which I knew Mt Pleasant Church provided, and I started to go with them.

I had been to Sunday Schools many times before, when I was a child. I had always been taught to 'do your best, and you'll go to heaven.' And so I did! Growing up, I always thought I was good enough, or at least, I wasn't too bad. But at this Sunday School, something was happening to me.

I couldn't say why, but I began to be deeply troubled in my heart. It was on hearing Bible verses which I had probably heard before but had no impact on me at first. Particular verses I remember include, *'Repent and be converted that your sins may be blotted out'* and *'Christ Jesus came into the world to save sinners.'* They sank deep into my ears and unsettled me in a way I couldn't explain. I know now that the Holy Spirit was bringing these words to me loud and clear, I couldn't help but hear them. I suppose the verses were troubling me because they were exposing the fact that, despite what I had thought, I had not turned away from my sins and I was not saved.

I continued to be affected by what I was hearing at the church for some months, but I didn't share my feelings with anyone. One evening, somewhat unexpectedly, I found myself in the church at the time when they met to pray! What had happened that day was this: I was deeply troubled in my heart again, crippled under the sense that I was a terrible sinner. Looking for help, I decided to speak with a friend of mine – her Dad was a pastor, so I figured she would know what I should do. She told me to speak to the pastor at the church here. Well, I was sure that if I told the pastor what was happening to me, he would think I was mad! But that night, I was so desperate nothing could have stopped me.

By some sort of irresistible grace, I was led down the hill to the church where the Christians were praying in their meeting. I openly confessed there that I believed that God had sent me there for help!

The people could see that the Lord was working in me. The pastor's wife and one of the elders kindly gave me space to talk with them in a side room and they prayed with me about all the things which had been bothering my heart.

I cried and I cried! I openly confessed that I was a sinner and asked the Lord for help. When we had finished praying, I told them that I felt an unfathomably deep peace inside myself, as if a huge weight had rolled off my shoulders. I knew that my sins were totally, fully, freely, finally, wonderfully forgiven.

The couple who helped me pray reminded me that it was like that old Christian story, *'Pilgrim's Progress.'* In that story, an agonised man called Christian prayed at the foot of Jesus' cross and his guilty burden rolled off his shoulders, never to be seen again.

That night, I knew for sure that the Lord had put my life on a different path. I was different. The Bible says that when we turn to Jesus we become *'a new creature in Christ,'* that's me. I felt deeply the truth and reality of those verses which had troubled me, and the relief of them too, that *'Jesus loved me and gave himself for me.'* I was certain of these things. But I will never understand why he has loved me, died for me, and forgiven me; why he was so patient in drawing me to him to give me new life.

For the first few months, I was worried that I wouldn't be able to keep up the new life he had given me. However, now I can look back over 45 years and see that it was the Lord who has been keeping me. I am so thankful to him for keeping me safe in him. Over the years, there have been many sad and difficult periods in my life, just like everyone else. Nevertheless, I have been so blessed with a loving family, many friends and the support of the three pastors I have had in my time. The church family have been an anchor through it all.

For anyone who is unsure or nervous about walking through the church doors for the first time, I would encourage you – give us a try! I am so glad that I did all those years ago. He saved me, blessed be his name.

Addiction Started To Break

'Mike Williams'

Maesycwmmer

The world really started to get a hold of me when I started comprehensive school. I saw the guys who seemed to have it all. They were tough, more popular, and they got all the girls. Everyone thought they were cool, and so did I. When they were getting into things like drink and drugs, I wanted to follow. I wanted to be like them – and that's exactly what happened. I became their friend, then I became just like them.

Drinking heavily and taking all sorts of drugs was normal to us, we smoked every day. Objectifying women was normal too and we would trade dirty videos regularly. It seemed like something I was in control of at the start but before long I was taking heavier and heavier drugs. Suddenly, I'm in my mid thirties and a helpless addict. Addicted to alcohol, drugs, empty weekends and random women. It wasn't a good life at all; I was controlled by my addictions, and I was in big trouble. Although I knew this, I would carry on and tell myself, 'Next week, I'll quit it all,' but I never would. I was *'like a dog returning to its own vomit.'*

Living this way was ruining my life. My physical and mental health suffered, I was severely stressed and anxious all the time. I worried my parents awfully and would bring trouble to their house. Mine was a selfish life which brought shame and distress to me and my family. I became really destructive too.

I had to look for hope. In my search, I came across 'New Age Spirituality.' It seemed to be what I was looking for. New Age Spirituality tried to teach me that humans are all one cosmic energy and spiritual beings enduring a temporary human experience. It said that there are no eternal consequences to how we live and that once we die, we get to come back and do it again.

This was so good to my ears since it gave me excuses for my behaviour, and I didn't really have to change. It let me fulfil the desires of my lusts all I liked, so I attached myself to this teaching and used psychedelic drugs to further advance my experiences.

One day, the floor fell out from under my world. After months of following this stuff, I was watching New Age videos online. On an automatic loop one would play after another without stopping. An hour into this binge, a video started to play which was of a different nature. It was a video of a man telling the good news about Jesus. He said that 2000 years ago, a man called Jesus claimed to be God, died on a cross for the sins of the world and rose again from the dead three days later.

The Christian message threw a spanner in the works of what I thought to be the truth! This news said that God is not just cosmic energy but a personal creator: a Father, Son and Spirit I can know. He is almighty and benevolent, and he requires a relationship with me. It said that humans aren't inconsequential but sinners, that none of us are good with God on our own. The message of Jesus told me that my sinful heart had opened a big void between me and the

Living God and there was nothing I could do to make it right.

It was an unsettling learning curve. I knew it was true. I knew I wasn't right with God and so had a feeling that if I was to die, it wouldn't be good for me. I knew that I would go to hell, completely separated from the God of life for all of eternity. Thankfully, there was hope in this message. Just as Jesus rose from the dead to new life, so could I. Just as he is alive today, so can I be through him. The good news about Jesus told me that if I would believe this man is God, that he really did die for me, and if I followed him, then all my sins would be forgiven, and I would be saved.

This was a completely different message to the New Age teachings. I had thought that there were many paths to God and even if we get it wrong then it's OK because we can just come back and try again in another life. This good news about Jesus told me there is only one way and that way is Jesus, and only Jesus.

The good news I heard through that video really stirred my soul and I knew it required action. Not long after watching it, after my heart trembled for a while, I did come to believe in Jesus and trust him with all my sins. The decision to follow Jesus is the best and the most important decision I've ever made. I found the true meaning of life, even everlasting life: to know God and to know his Son Jesus, to have a relationship with him.

Through Jesus' power and help, I learned to repent and turn my back on the old life. The chains of addiction started to break. It wasn't all at once, but as time went on, I was being set free from my sins. I am not without sin, but I am free from it. I am *'no longer a slave to sin, but a slave to righteousness.'* Only by the grace of God was this possible. The Bible says, *'if anyone is in Christ, he is a new creation. The old has passed away. Behold, all things have become new.'* I am proof of this! The old me is dead, *'it is no longer I who live, but Christ that lives in me.'* This is what it means to be born again. Hallelujah! What a Saviour is Jesus!

We all bow the knee and worship something, whether we believe in God or not. Before, my god was sinful living. I was looking for comfort, peace and joy in these things but all it did was leave me more empty and looking for more. Being where I am now, I know that it is only Jesus that can fulfil and satisfy us. Everything else leaves us lost and empty *for the wages of sin is death, but the gift of God is eternal life in Christ Jesus our Lord.*

I Wouldn't Have Coped

Jill Jones

Maesycwmmer

I've had a few problems in the last 18 years and I know, I know, that without God I wouldn't be have coped. So…here I am…at last.

We Went To Say Goodbye

Heddwen George

Maesycwmmer

I grew up in an idyllic little village in the heart of Snowdonia, North Wales; one of those tourist hot-spots in the summer. Had you asked me, I'd have said that the life I had was perfect! I had a happy home, three fun brothers, good friends and the great and gorgeous outdoors. There were only four of us in my class at school and I seem to remember spending most of the time having adventures anyway.

My parents were Christians, and we all went to church every Sunday. I loved it, church is a great place for children to grow up. At home, my brothers and I were taught right from wrong and how to behave well, so I always thought I was 'one of the good ones.' All this meant I was perfectly at peace inside and out. I had a really happy life, and not a care in the world.

Then it all went horribly wrong. When I was 6 years old, I felt like my childhood was over. My oldest brother, Elgan, was diagnosed with a life-threatening brain tumour. He was 15 years old at the time and needed urgent surgery to try and save his life. We had to move far away, to the city, for access to bigger hospitals and to be closer to extended family. I changed home, schools, church and, well, everything. Nothing was the same.

One day, my other brothers and I were brought to visit Elgan in hospital, to say goodbye. The brain surgery he was due to have was so risky that he might not make it through the operation. I was so scared to see my brother; I was especially frightened to see him weak or frightened. I didn't want to see that. But it wasn't like that at all.

My brother was brimming with inexplicable peace. This was not what I had expected at all! Facing the end of his life, Elgan told me that he had put his trust in Jesus and so, alive or dead, he was at peace. He said that he was happy to either live for Jesus or die and be with Jesus.

Because I had always gone to church, I knew these truths in my head. I believed there was a God, that there was a heaven and hell, that Jesus died on the cross to take away sins and the rest of it. But my brother showed me that knowing *about* God was not enough, I needed to know and trust him.

My life didn't change dramatically from that point, but the niggling feeling stayed with me. I realised that if I swapped places with Elgan, and it was me with the cancer, I was not ready to meet Jesus. I did not have Jesus' peace in the face of death.

While this lingered in my mind, I thought to do something about it. I kept going to church. I kept learning more about God. I tried being a better person, I tried to be good. I tried praying and reading my Bible more too. In short, I tried to fix myself, do it myself and work my way to God. It didn't work. I had yet to see that going to church and trying to be good didn't make me right with God at all.

Over the next few years, the Holy Spirit showed me that the sin which the Bible talked about was in MY heart - and I couldn't fix it myself. So, I finally gave up. I confessed my sins to Jesus and said sorry for all the wrong things I'd done and thought. I trusted that when Jesus died on the cross, it was for ME and my sins. That's when I truly became a Christian. All the theory in my head entered my heart, he saved me, gave me new life, peace hope, faith. I had really hoped for a special fuzzy feeling that some Christians talk about. But everyone is different, and that didn't happen to me. And because I had always lived like a Christian my lifestyle didn't change drastically. What had changed was my heart, it was full of my brother's peace as I was trusting Jesus.

I remember clinging to Romans 10:9 *'if you confess with your mouth the Lord Jesus and believe in your heart that God has raised him from the dead you WILL be saved.'* I confessed the Lord Jesus, I believed in his resurrection from the dead and so I trusted that the Lord had saved me.

It's been 12 years since then, and the same things are true. I keep bringing my guilt and sin to Jesus and he just keeps on forgiving me as I repent and trust in him. Praise him! For me, it is no longer a fruitless head knowledge which leaves me peaceless and afraid. It's no longer merely learning more about God without knowing him. For me, it's getting to know my Saviour Jesus Christ more and more. For me, *'to live is Christ, and to die is gain.'*

A Place For Me

John Price

Ystrad Mynach

From as young an age as I can remember, I was always sent off to church every Sunday by my family. I heard so many Bible stories over the years, but I never really understood what they meant, or what they had to do with one another, or me! As soon as I was a teenager and able to decide for myself, I stopped going. None of my friends kept going, it wasn't cool, so we all stopped.

When I turned 16 years old, I started to study Typing and Commerce at Ystrad Further Education College. Since then, it's become Coleg y Cymoedd and still offers further education to a lot of young adults to give them a bright future. I'd never have guessed the future which was in front of me when I enrolled there!

On my very first day in college, I went to the canteen for lunch. I didn't really know anybody, but found myself sitting next to a boy a similar age to me, who happened to be a Christian. And by that, I mean, he had heard the same stories I always had, but he had come to understand what they were all about. Over lunch, he told me about Jesus.

He said that Jesus Christ had died on the cross as a substitute for sinners like me. He said that Jesus had risen from the dead three days later to prove what he had done.

This short encounter had a profound impact on me, even though I had heard the story many times before. This time, it wriggled into my heart. Later, I found out that some Christians were meeting in Caerphilly every Saturday evening, and I wanted to join them. I went along to hear the messages from the Bible about Jesus and how he had died to save people like me from sin, death and hell. The leader of that particular group invited me to come to Mt Pleasant Church in Maesycwmmer, since it was closer to me than Caerphilly, where I learned more about the Bible week by week.

Some things are always the same when people tell the stories of how they became Christians, such as the centrality of Jesus and his cross. But some things are often different, such as the timings. Like many, I don't know exactly when it happened to me, but over a certain period of time I came to believe this wonderful, good news! I became sure that Jesus had died for ME. He was MY Saviour.

That was many years ago now and the Lord has always been there for me. While there is a lot of uncertainty in life, especially these days, I am convinced of these three things:

1. All my sins have been graciously forgiven.
2. The penalty for my sins has been paid once, for all and forever, by Jesus Christ.

Because of this, he has reserved a place for me with him, in heaven.

Epilogue

When I read these stories myself, they reminded me of the story told in the Bible of a man named Nicodemus. In his own eyes, and the opinion of others, Nicodemus appeared to have his life together, but Jesus told him that he needed an entirely new life – a life so radically different that Jesus described it as *'a new birth which comes from above'* – a total spiritual transformation without which Nicodemus would never see or enter the kingdom of God.

It might have hurt, but the truth does that sometimes. Jesus told Nicodemus that he needed God to give him new birth as a gift, for just as Nicodemus could not give himself natural birth, so he could not give himself this spiritual, new birth.

You may be wondering how you may experience this new birth, this new life which Jesus spoke about and local people here have experienced. Well, just as your natural birth depended upon the initiative of others (your Dad and Mam) in a similar manner we need someone else to take the initative and give us new spiritual life, new birth. The initiative lies with the Living God. So, we must ask him to give this gift.

Do not doubt his willingness to hear you and to give you this gift of new life. The Living God has promised that if we truly seek him we shall find him.

You will seek me and find me when you seek me with all your heart.

Jeremiah 29:13

Printed in Great Britain
by Amazon